Carbohydrates

George Ivanoff

Smart Apple Media
P.O. Box 3263
Mankato, MN, 56002

First published in 2011 by
MACMILLAN EDUCATION AUSTRALIA PTY LTD
15–19 Claremont St, South Yarra, Australia 3141

Visit our web site at www.macmillan.com.au or go directly to www.macmillanlibrary.com.au

Associated companies and representatives throughout the world.

Library of Congress Cataloging-in-Publication Data has been applied for.

Publisher: Carmel Heron
Commissioning Editor: Niki Horin
Managing Editor: Vanessa Lanaway
Editor: Emma Short
Proofreader: Georgina Garner
Designer: Kerri Wilson
Page layout: Cath Pirret Design
Photo researcher: Sarah Johnson (management: Debbie Gallagher)
Illustrator: Leigh Hedstrom, Flee Illustration
Production Controller: Vanessa Johnson

Manufactured in China by Macmillan Production (Asia) Ltd.
Kwun Tong, Kowloon, Hong Kong
Supplier Code: CP December 2010

Acknowledgments

The author and the publisher are grateful to the following for permission to reproduce copyright material:

Front cover photograph: Boy eating sandwich, Corbis/Blend Images/Jose Luis Pelaez

Photographs courtesy of: Dreamstime/Ackleyroadphotos, 12 (orange), /Andresr, 22 (bread), /Cybernesco, 7 (middle), /Danako, 22 (honey), /Dawnbal1, 8, /De-kay, 19 (milk), /Digitoll, 16-17 (white rice), /Gelpi, 28, /Grusvag, 11, /Hkratky, 22 (fruit), /Icefront, 7 (bottom left), /Jlvdream, 16 (apple), /Karandaev, 17 (white bread), /Martijnmulder, 13 (vegetables), /Monkey Business Images, 24 (left), /Phoric, 16-17 (brown rice), /Picstudio, 24 (right), /Rimglow, 12 (sugar), 16 (milk & sugar), /Robynmac, 19 (fruit), /San32, 19 (nuts), /Tarczas, 17 (wholemeal bread), /Travismanley, 9 (right), /Tysmith, 12 (milk), 22 (milk), /Ukrphoto, 6 (bottom), /Valentyn75, 7 (bottom right); Getty Images/Meiko Arquillos, 26; iStockphoto, 30, /David Elfstrom, 21; Photolibrary/Imagesource, 29, /Monkey Business Images Ltd, 25, /Science Photo Library, 10; Pixmac/a4stockphotos, 6 (top), /Alexander Silaev, 7 (top); Shutterstock/Jacek Chabraszewski, 18, /Golden Pixels LLC, 4, /Monkey Business Images, 20, /Morgan Lane Photography, 3, 6 (middle), /naluwan, 5, / Cheryl Ann Quigley, 15, /Arek Rainczuk, 13 (grains), /Yanas, 16 (honey).

While every care has been taken to trace and acknowledge copyright, the publisher tenders their apologies for any accidental infringement where copyright has proved untraceable. They would be pleased to come to a suitable arrangement with the rightful owner in each case.

Contents

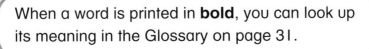

When a word is printed in **bold**, you can look up its meaning in the Glossary on page 31.

What's in My Food?

Your food is made up of **nutrients**. Nutrients help your body work, grow, and stay alive.

Nutrients give you **energy** so you can be active.

Different types of food contain different types of nutrients. A **balanced diet** includes foods with the right amount of nutrients for your body.

A balanced diet helps keep your body healthy.

What Nutrients Are in My Food?

There are many different types of nutrients in your food. They include proteins, carbohydrates, fats, fiber, minerals, and vitamins.

Protein in meat, poultry, eggs, and fish helps your body grow and heal.

Carbohydrates in bread and pasta give your body energy.

Fats in fish and olive oil give your body energy and help it stay healthy.

Fiber in bread and vegetables helps your body **digest** food.

Vitamins in fruit and vegetables help your body work well.

Minerals in milk and meat help your body grow and stay healthy.

Carbohydrates

Carbohydrates are nutrients that are in many foods. They give your body the energy it needs to be active every day.

Eating an apple as a snack is a great way to get carbohydrates.

Different types of food have different amounts of carbohydrates. Foods that contain a lot of **processed** sugar have a lot of carbohydrates. They are not always good for you.

Some foods with carbohydrates are good for you, but others are not.

Fruit, vegetables, and milk are good for you.

Candy and soft drinks are not good for you.

What Are Carbohydrates?

Carbohydrates are made up of smaller parts called **molecules**. Carbohydrate molecules contain **carbon**, **hydrogen**, and **oxygen**. You need a microscope to see them.

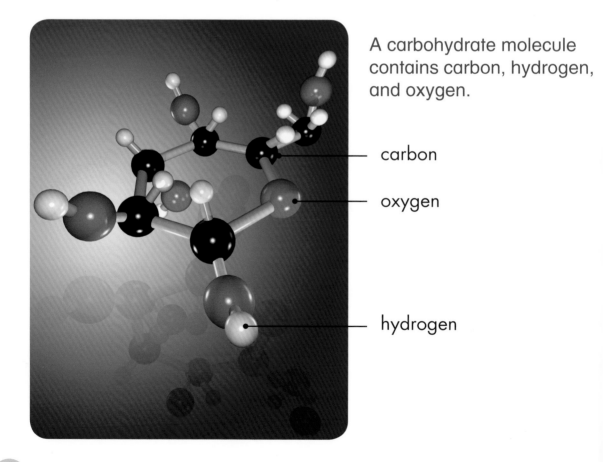

A carbohydrate molecule contains carbon, hydrogen, and oxygen.

carbon

oxygen

hydrogen

Carbohydrates are **macronutrients**. Your body needs a lot of macronutrients to stay healthy. There are two types of carbohydrates: simple carbohydrates and complex carbohydrates. Fats and protein are also macronutrients.

carbohydrates

protein

fats

Carbohydrates, as well as proteins and fats, can be found in hamburgers and chips.

Simple Carbohydrates

Simple carbohydrates are sugars called fructose, sucrose, and lactose. They are easy and quick to digest.

Processed sugar contains sucrose.

Fruit contains fructose.

Milk contains lactose.

Fruit, milk, and processed sugar contain simple carbohydrates that can be digested quickly.

Complex Carbohydrates

Complex carbohydrates are slower and harder to digest than simple carbohydrates. The energy from complex carbohydrates lasts longer than the energy from simple carbohydrates.

vegetables

grains

Vegetables and grains contain complex carbohydrates that are slow to digest.

How Does My Body Get Carbohydrates?

Your body **absorbs** carbohydrates when you digest food. When food breaks down in your stomach, the carbohydrates break into smaller parts. Your **liver** turns them into **glucose**.

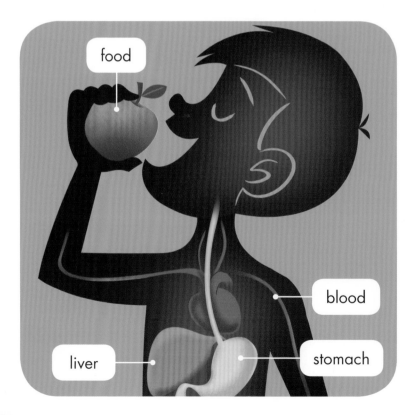

food

blood

liver

stomach

Glucose enters the blood, and your blood carries it all around your body.

Your body uses glucose to make energy. Glucose that is not used immediately is stored in your liver or your **muscles**. It can also be stored in **fatty tissue**.

Stored glucose can be used later, when your body needs more energy.

The Glycemic Index

The glycemic index, or GI, measures how quickly carbohydrates are absorbed by your body. Your body absorbs carbohydrates with a low GI more slowly than those with a high GI.

Low GI foods are better for your body because the energy they give you lasts longer.

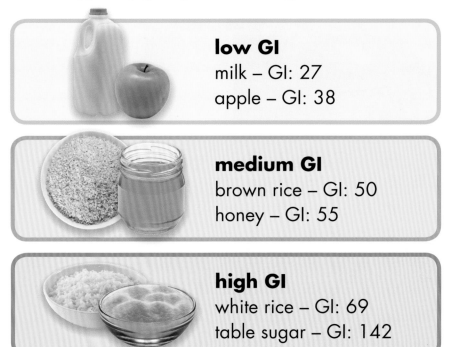

low GI
milk – GI: 27
apple – GI: 38

medium GI
brown rice – GI: 50
honey – GI: 55

high GI
white rice – GI: 69
table sugar – GI: 142

Processed foods, such as white bread and rice, often contain carbohydrates with a high GI, such as sugar. They also have less fiber than foods that are less processed.

High GI foods	Low GI foods
white bread	whole-grain bread
white rice	brown rice

Fiber can lower a food's GI. A low GI is healthier than a high GI.

What Do Carbohydrates Do?

Carbohydrates give you energy. They power your brain and also help protect your muscles.

Carbohydrates give you the energy you need to run and play.

Carbohydrates Power My Body

Carbohydrates help your body move, work, and stay active. Most of your body's energy comes from carbohydrates.

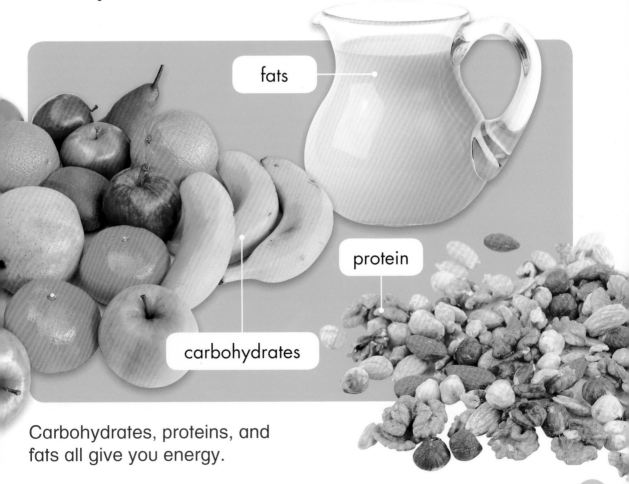

fats

protein

carbohydrates

Carbohydrates, proteins, and fats all give you energy.

Carbohydrates Power My Brain

Your brain needs energy from carbohydrates to work well. Carbohydrates help you concentrate and think.

Your body needs carbohydrates to help you learn.

Carbohydrates Keep Me Strong

Your body needs carbohydrates to protect your muscles. Without energy from carbohydrates, it would use the protein in your muscles for energy instead. This would make your muscles waste away.

Carbohydrates give your body energy so it doesn't break down protein in your muscles.

Which Foods Contain Carbohydrates?

Lots of foods contain carbohydrates. Different foods have different types of carbohydrates and different GI levels. You need to eat foods that contain carbohydrates every day.

bread

milk

honey

fruit

These foods contain different kinds of carbohydrates.

Foods with carbohydrates are part of a balanced diet. Other foods also have nutrients that your body needs, such as vitamins and minerals. You need to eat these foods, too.

A balanced diet includes many different kinds of foods, as well as water.

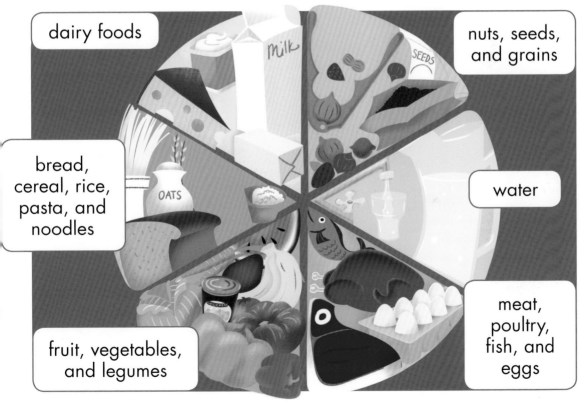

dairy foods

nuts, seeds, and grains

bread, cereal, rice, pasta, and noodles

water

fruit, vegetables, and legumes

meat, poultry, fish, and eggs

Carbohydrates Are in Fruit and Vegetables

Fruit and vegetables contain carbohydrates.
Some have a low GI, and some have a high GI.
Fruit and vegetables also have other nutrients that
your body needs.

Potatoes have a high GI and apples have a low GI.

Carbohydrates Are in Sweets

Candies, cakes, and soft drinks contain carbohydrates. These types of foods have a lot of sugar and are low in other nutrients.

Eating too many sweet foods is not good for your body.

Carbohydrates Are in Grains

Grains, such as wheat, rice, and barley, contain carbohydrates. These grains are used to make bread, pasta, and breakfast cereals.

Some breakfast cereals have a low GI and also contain protein.

White bread is made with processed grains. It has a higher GI than whole-grain bread, which is made with whole grains that are not processed.

When a grain is processed, the germ and bran are removed. These parts contain the best nutrients.

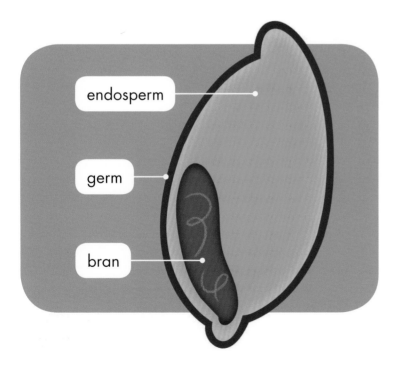

endosperm

germ

bran

Carbohydrates Are in Dairy Foods

Dairy foods are made from milk. Yogurt and cheese are dairy foods. All of these foods contain carbohydrates and a low GI.

Dairy foods also contain a mineral called calcium, which keeps your bones and teeth healthy.

Some dairy products, such as ice cream and flavored yogurt, have large amounts of sugar. These types of foods are not very good for you.

Carbohydrates in milk are good for you, but the sugar in flavored milk is not.

What Happens if I Don't Eat Carbohydrates?

If you don't eat carbohydrates, you will not have the energy to run or play. You will not be able to concentrate or learn. Your muscles will waste away.

If you don't eat carbohydrates, your body will not have enough energy to be active.

Body will have no energy.

Muscles will become weak.

Glossary

absorbs	takes in
balanced diet	a healthy selection of food that you eat
carbon	a gas in the air
digest	to break down food in the body
energy	the ability to be active
fatty tissue	parts of the body where fat is stored
glucose	a sugar in your body
hydrogen	a gas in the air
liver	the part of your body that makes glucose
macronutrients	nutrients that your body needs a lot of
molecules	very small parts in food
muscles	parts of the body that help you move
nutrients	the healthy parts of food that people need to live
oxygen	a gas in the air that living things need to breathe
processed	changed in some way

Index